SUCCESSFUL AMERICANS

Arab Americans

William Mark Habeeb

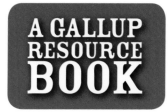

A GALLUP RESOURCE BOOK

Mason Crest Publishers
Philadelphia

Produced by OTTN Publishing in association with
Bow Publications, Inc.

MASON CREST PUBLISHERS INC.
370 Reed Road
Broomall, Pennsylvania 19008
(866) MCP-BOOK (toll free)
www.masoncrest.com

Printed in the United States of America.

First Printing

9 8 7 6 5 4 3 2 1

Library of Congress Cataloging-in-Publication Data

Habeeb, William Mark, 1955–
  Arab Americans / William Mark Habeeb.
    p. cm. — (Successful Americans)
  Includes bibliographical references and index.
  ISBN 978-1-4222-0514-3 (hardcover)
  ISBN 978-1-4222-0854-0 (pbk.)
  1. Arab Americans—Biography—Juvenile literature. 2. Successful people—United
States—Biography—Juvenile literature. I. Title.
  E184.A65H33 2009
  305.892'70730922—dc22
  [B]
                                                                    2008042537

Publisher's note:
All quotations in this book come from original sources, and contain the spelling
and grammatical inconsistencies of the original text.

◀ **CROSS-CURRENTS** ▶

When you see this logo, turn
to the Cross-Currents section
at the back of the book. The
Cross-Currents features explore
connections between people,
places, events, and ideas.

Table of Contents

"Don't forget your folks at home"

The story of Bashara Kalil Forzley (B.K.) is typical of many Arabs who immigrated to the United States during the Great Migration. He came to find work to support his family back home. Upon arrival, other relatives who had already immigrated here helped him settle in. Later, B.K. brought other members of his family to the United States. The process of bringing relatives one after the other is known as "chain migration."

B.K. was born in 1883 in Karoun, a town in modern day Lebanon. As he got older, his father was unable to work the family farm and when B.K. turned 14, his mother sent him to America to find work. B.K.'s cousin had already immigrated to the U.S. and settled in Worcester, Massachusetts. Upon B.K.'s departure, his mother pinned his cousin's address to B.K.'s jacket. As he set off from Beirut in 1897, his mother gave him this advice, "Always associate yourself with people who are your elders, do not indulge in liquor, smoking, dating or partying, and do not forget your folks at home. If you live and succeed we also will succeed by our manifested happiness."

That same year, ... brother Abra... In 1908, B.K. wen... ...d married Alma... parents were already ... a. The two sailed to ... arrived at Ellis Island...

B.K. and Almaza settled in Worcester among the Syrian co... They named their son "Victor" after the American victory in W... War I. B.K. stayed in touch with his family in Lebanon and visited several times. He also donated generously to his native village of Karoun. In 1958, B.K. published his autobiography — biogr...

An exhibit from the Arab American National Museum. Located in Dearborn, Michigan, the museum features information on the history, culture, and contributions of the 3.5 million people in the United States who trace their ancestry to the Arab world.

CHAPTER ONE

Arab Immigration to America

A rab immigrants first came to shores of the United States in the late 19th century. Like all immigrants, they were attracted by the lure of America's promise and the prospect of better lives. At the time, most of the Arab world was under the control of the Turkish Ottoman Empire, which had ruled over a vast territory in the Middle East and North Africa since 1299.

FIRST WAVE OF IMMIGRATION

The vast majority of early Arab immigrants to America came from what is today Lebanon, Syria, and Palestine. About 90 percent of them were Christians—either Roman Catholic or Eastern Orthodox. Many were fleeing religious persecution by Muslims and the heavy hand of Ottoman rule. Others hoped to escape economic distress due to overpopulation: there simply was not enough agricultural land to accommodate all of the people, most of whom were farmers.

In the early 1900s Lebanon and Syria suffered a devastating famine in which thousands of people starved to death. When World War I broke out in 1914, the Ottoman rulers imposed heavy taxes on their Arab subjects and conscripted young men into the Ottoman Army. During the war immigration was impossible, but as soon as the conflict ended, in 1918, immigration soared. Overall, from 1880 to 1924, an estimated 150,000 Arabs immigrated to the United States.

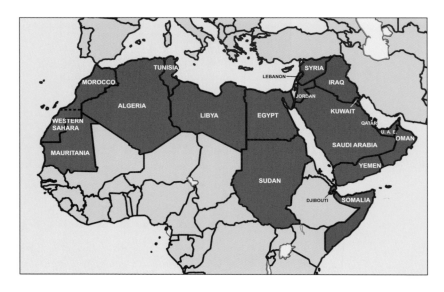

The Arab world, shown in red, refers to countries in which the predominant language is Arabic. It includes nations in northern Africa and southwestern Asia.

A NEW LIFE IN AMERICA

Most early Arab immigrants were poorly educated. They had survived for generations by subsistence farming. Lacking the money to buy farmland in America, they had to seek new sources of income. Initially, Arab immigrants settled in major cities, especially New York, as well as in New England factory towns. They worked in textile mills or sold goods door-to-door. Eventually, some families saved enough to open small dry goods shops (selling textiles, clothing, and other non-food items) and grocery stores. Life was hard: Families usually lived above their stores, and everyone—including children—was required to work.

In time some Arab immigrants began to migrate out of the big cities to smaller communities in Pennsylvania, West Virginia, and Ohio. By around 1920 nearly 25 percent of Arab immigrants lived in the American South, especially in Louisiana, Texas, and Mississippi.

Many earned money by peddling household goods in rural regions. Peddling involved traveling on foot from one small town to the next and selling goods from a pushcart or large sack. During the 1920s Arab peddlers became a common sight on the back roads of rural America. Over time the more successful peddlers settled in one place as suppliers and shopkeepers.

Early Arab immigrants faced many of the same challenges as other immigrants: They had little knowledge of English, possessed meager financial resources, and often encountered prejudice. Because Arabs tended to have darker complexions than European immigrants, they were targets of racial prejudice. For example, both Georgia and South Carolina attempted to deny Arabs the right to naturalization as American citizens on the grounds that Arabs were not truly "white."

Arabs responded to such discrimination by working hard at assimilation. They often changed their names to make them sound more "American," and they encouraged their children to excel in school as a means of improving their lives.

BECOMING AMERICANS

In the 1930s the U.S. passed strict new immigration laws. By this time the early Arab immigrants were already established. Their American-born children felt equal to other Americans

Syrian children work at harvesting cranberries at the Maple Park Bog, in East Wareham, Massachusetts, in this 1911 photograph by Lewis Wickes Hines.

and sought the same opportunities. The immigrants' emphasis on education had begun to pay off, and increasingly their children were pursuing professional careers.

While Arab families became assimilated in American society, they also made efforts to maintain their culture. This was achieved largely through preserving traditional Arabic cuisine and participating within churches and social clubs. For example, Lebanese immigrants established social groups often known as "Cedars Clubs" (after the famous cedar trees of Lebanon). The Arabic language, however, fell out of use among most Arabs who were born in America. While the parents typically spoke Arabic to each other, they encouraged their children to use English.

SECOND AND THIRD WAVES OF IMMIGRATION
A second wave of Arab immigration began after World War II (1940–1945), when immigration laws were relaxed and American industry sought laborers. A majority of this second wave of

The Islamic Center and Mosque in Cedar Rapids, Iowa, completed in 1972. A small number of Muslims settled in Cedar Rapids at the turn of the 20th century; however, most Arab Americans in the early 1900s were Christians.

new immigrants were Muslims, although Arab Christians continued to enter the United States as well. Large numbers came from Palestine, Egypt, Yemen, and Iraq, as well as Lebanon and Syria. The immigrants took factory jobs in such cities as Chicago, Illinois, and Cleveland, Ohio. A large Arab community was established in the Detroit area, where automobile plants offered many jobs.

In the 1970s a new wave of immigration from the Middle East began, sparked by regional conflicts. These new immigrants tended to be better educated than the early immigrants; frequently, they were professionals or scholars. Some came to the United States as university students and chose to remain. This third wave of Arab immigrants commonly settled in urban areas or college towns.

CHALLENGES FACED BY ARAB AMERICANS

Every immigrant group has faced challenges. It is not unusual for one or two generations to pass before an immigrant community feels fully assimilated into American life. Arab Americans, however, have faced some unique challenges.

Early Arab immigrants to the United States were mostly Christian. Because that is the majority religion in the United States, these early immigrants were accepted by other Americans. But many of them faced the same racism and discrimination encountered by black Americans in 20th century America.

Arab Americans also suffered from negative perceptions of their native lands. The Arab world is poorly understood in the United States, and Arabs were often portrayed negatively

◄ **CROSS-CURRENTS** ►

In June 2006 respondents to a Gallup poll gave their opinions about the number of immigrants entering the United States from Arab countries: 39 percent said "too many," 12 percent reported "too few," 38 percent said "about right," while 10 percent had no opinion. To see how Americans' opinions on overall immigration have changed over the years, turn to page 50.

in Hollywood films and on television. In addition, many Arab states have been in conflict with Israel, a close U.S. ally. This hostility has led to negative stereotypes of all Arabs.

In reaction, Arab Americans, like many other ethnic and immigrant groups, have established organizations to combat negative stereotypes and call attention to overt prejudice. The Arab-American Anti-Discrimination Committee (ADC) and the Arab American Institute (AAI), for example, have done much to raise awareness of prejudice against Arab Americans.

THE IMPACT OF TERRORISM

On September 11, 2001, terrorists hijacked three commercial airliners and flew them into New York's World Trade Center and the Pentagon in Washington. A fourth hijacked plane crashed in Pennsylvania. Altogether, more than 3,000 people were killed.

Because the hijackers were Arab Muslims, Arab Americans were subjected to threats, racist remarks, and even physical attack during the weeks that followed. Many Arab-American Muslims pulled their children out of school to prevent them from being humiliated or attacked. Others went into hiding. Some Arab Americans found themselves subject to extra scrutiny when attempting to board airplanes, and in several instances Arab Americans were barred from taking a flight because of their ethnicity.

A BRIGHT FUTURE

In dealing with the terrorist attacks of September 11, the Arab-American community has sought to reach out to others in the United States. That experience has strengthened the group, whose numbers are estimated at 3.5 million. Only about a quarter of Arab Americans are Muslim; more than half are Catholic or Eastern Orthodox.

ATTITUDES TOWARD MUSLIM ARABS

The terrorist attacks of September 11, 2001, and increased political violence around the world have resulted in increased prejudice and discrimination against Muslims and Arabs. In a July 2006 Gallup poll, 39 percent of Americans admitted to holding prejudice against Muslims. Some said that certain measures should be put in place, such as requiring all Muslims—U.S. citizens included—to carry special IDs.

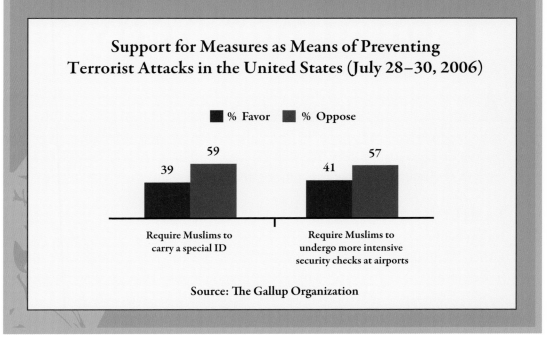

Support for Measures as Means of Preventing Terrorist Attacks in the United States (July 28–30, 2006)

■ % Favor   ■ % Oppose

| Require Muslims to carry a special ID | Require Muslims to undergo more intensive security checks at airports |

39   59   41   57

Source: The Gallup Organization

From the earliest days, Arab Americans have contributed to building a better United States. And as a community that emphasizes the merits of education, hard work, and a strong family, Arab Americans likely will continue to enrich American society for years to come.

CHAPTER TWO

Ralph Nader: Consumer Activist

A uthor and political activist Ralph Nader is the first and only Arab American ever to run for the office of president of the United States. This son of Lebanese immigrants is well known for his efforts over the years to fight for consumer rights and safety. He has led many other activists to work to influence issues in areas such as consumer safety, energy, and the environment.

FAMILY ROOTS

Ralph Nader was born in Winsted, Connecticut, on February 27, 1934. Ralph's father, Nathra, had immigrated to the United States in 1912 from a small village in Lebanon. For eight years Nathra Nader worked in factories and textile mills in various cities, saving his money. In 1920 he returned to Lebanon, where he married Rose, a village schoolteacher. In 1925 the couple immigrated to the United States permanently.

The Naders settled in the small town of Winsted, where Nathra opened a candy store on Winsted's main street. It soon grew to become a full-service restaurant. It also became the central meeting place for people who wanted to discuss, or argue over, politics and civic life.

Nathra Nader was intensely interested in the political issues of the day, and he taught his children to be inquisitive and to take a stand. As Nader later recalled, "One day, when I was about ten, I came home from grade school. When my father saw me, he asked a simple question: 'What did you learn today Ralph? Did you learn how to believe or did you learn how to think?'"

Nightly debates took place at the Nader dinner table, as parents and children argued and discussed a range of issues. Although neither of Ralph's parents were college educated, they read widely and encouraged their children to think independently. "If we wanted to be leaders," Nader recalled, "we were taught that we would have to be willing to be different."

COMMITMENT TO CHANGE

Nader was an excellent student, and he determined at an early age that becoming a lawyer would be the best way to fight for changes in society. After graduating from high school in 1951, he attended Princeton University, in New Jersey, and Harvard

Ralph Nader has worked for decades as an advocate to ensure that consumer goods and services are safe, environmentally friendly, and of good quality. When asked to define himself, he always responds, "Full-time citizen, the most important office in America for anyone to achieve."

On May 12, 1966, Nader appears at a Senate hearing called after publication of Unsafe at Any Speed. *As a result of his book, a series of automobile safety laws were passed the same year.*

Law School, in Cambridge, Massachusetts, and graduated with honors. In the late 1950s he started a small law practice. However, his real interest lay in speaking out against American corporations that were abusing the rights and safety of consumers.

In 1965 Nader published the book *Unsafe at Any Speed*. It detailed how the major automobile companies were producing vehicles that were not safe (at the time, cars did not come with seat belts, air bags, and other safety equipment). *Unsafe at Any Speed* became an immediate best-seller. Public interest sparked Congressional investigations into automobile safety. The book and subsequent articles and speeches helped push through new laws requiring automobile companies to improve vehicle safety. The 31-year-old son of Lebanese immigrants had taken on the powerful automobile industry—and won.

THE FIRST "CONSUMER ADVOCATE"

Nader had invented a new career—the "consumer advocate." He decided to devote his life to fighting for the average

American by exposing dangers and injustices. The 1960s were an era of great social unrest and activism, and Nader soon put together a team of young lawyers and researchers. They became known as Nader's Raiders for their relentless investigation into unsafe products, pollution, corporate crime, and the lack of government regulation to ensure consumer safety.

Nader and his Raiders were responsible for dozens of new laws and regulations. These consumer advocates also played a role in the creation of several new government agencies, including the Environmental Protection Agency (EPA) and the Consumer Product Safety Commission.

RUNNING FOR PRESIDENT

By the 1980s Nader had succeeded in creating dozens of activist organizations to fight for important consumer issues. He continued to direct the activities of his original organization, Public Citizen (founded in 1971), but he turned over leadership of other groups he had founded to those who had come to work for him. As one of the most popular speakers in America, Nader spent much of his time traveling to college campuses, rallies, and other public appearances.

During the mid-1990s Nader came to believe that the two major political parties—the Democrats and the Republicans—were not going to bring about the changes he believed in. He saw them as beholden to big corporations, in part because the two parties raised millions of dollars from corporate donors for election campaigns. Nader concluded that there was very little difference between the two major parties on the issues that were most important to him. These issues included universal health care, a reduction of excessive military spending, and elimination of what he saw as corporate greed.

To bring attention to the causes in which he believed, Nader entered the political process. In 1996 he ran for president

Nader has moved beyond social criticism to political action by entering several U.S. presidential races. As a Green Party candidate in 2000 he campaigns in New York.

of the United States as the candidate of the Green Party, which promoted ecological and environmental issues. But he did not campaign widely and had very limited resources.

THE CONTROVERSIAL 2000 ELECTION

In 2000 Nader decided to campaign more seriously, once again as the Green Party candidate. He argued that there was very little difference between the Republican candidate, George W. Bush, and the Democratic candidate, Al Gore. Nader campaigned aggressively and won nearly 3 million votes—just under 3 percent of the total votes cast.

Normally, a third party candidate who receives less than 3 percent of the vote is not a major factor in an election. But 2000 was different. The presidential race between Bush and Gore was the closest in U.S. history, and just a few hundred votes in the state of Florida accounted for Bush's victory. Democrats were furious at Ralph Nader. They argued that had he stayed out of the race—a race that he had no chance of winning—Gore would have won.

The Democrats based this argument on the belief that most of the votes Nader received in Florida would have gone to Gore if Nader had not been on the ballot. Nader and his supporters, however, responded that many people would not have voted at all had his name not been on the ballot. He refused to take responsibility for Gore's defeat.

In 2004 Nader ran again for the presidency, although many Democrats tried to persuade him not to. Nader's response was true to his beliefs:

> Voting for a candidate of one's choice is a Constitutional right, and the Democrats who are asking me not to run are, without question, seeking to deny the Constitutional rights of voters who are, by law, otherwise free to choose to vote for me.

Nader entered the presidential race again in 2008. He refused to give up his right to debate the issues, and he refused to deny his supporters the right to vote for him. Nader has written, "My father used to say, 'If you do not use your rights, you will lose your rights.'" The values of Nader's immigrant parents were so instrumental in forming the man he became that he wrote a book called *The Seventeen Traditions*. It tells about his childhood and the lessons he learned from his parents.

◀ CROSS-CURRENTS ▶

Immigrants to the United States often remain connected to their native country when they have relatives back in the "old country." Ralph Nader and his siblings learned a great deal about their parent's homeland of Lebanon. To find out how, turn to page 52.

Ralph Nader: Consumer Activist

CHAPTER THREE

Donna Shalala: Secretary of Health and Human Services

The granddaughter of Lebanese immigrants, Donna Shalala has served in many leadership positions. One of the most important was that of Secretary of Health and Human Services, a position she held for eight years during the 1990s, in the administration of President Bill Clinton. Shalala is the first Arab American to serve in a president's cabinet. She is also an accomplished scholar and teacher.

EARLY YEARS

Donna Shalala and her twin sister, Diane, were born in Cleveland, Ohio, on February 14, 1941. At the time Cleveland and its suburbs had a well-established Arab-American community, and the Shalala family was an important part of it.

Donna's grandparents had immigrated to the area from Lebanon, and her parents were hard-working professionals. Her father was a realtor and her mother was a tax attorney. While her two daughters were young, Donna's mother had enrolled in law school and in 1952 established a career. This was a radical step for a woman in that era, and the message was not lost on Donna: She learned from her mother to accept no limits to her ambition or her dreams.

Secretary of Health and Human Services Donna Shalala meets with President Bill Clinton and Vice President Al Gore to discuss current developments in AIDS research. The poster, which reads "One World, One Hope" marked World AIDS Day, held on December 1, 1996.

Shalala's resolve was evident from an early age. In the summer of 1951, when she was 10 years old, Donna played softball in a summer youth league. Her team was coached by a young college student, who at first refused to play Shalala at first base, her preferred position. But in the face of Donna's persistent demands, the coach finally relented. "What she lacked in size, she made up for in feistiness," said the coach, George Steinbrenner. He would become well known himself, as the owner of the New York Yankees.

SERVICE IN THE PEACE CORPS

Shalala's parents strongly encouraged their daughter to go to college and pursue a professional life. She attended Western College for Women, in Oxford, Ohio. When she graduated in 1962, she was ready for a break from school—but not from learning.

Shalala joined the Peace Corps and for two years served in Iran—at the time a U.S. ally—where she helped to build and establish an agricultural college. Her family was initially unenthusiastic about their daughter living so far away from Cleveland. Her father, Shalala later said, tried to bribe her to stay home. But her elderly grandmother knew there was no way to stop her. Instead, she gave Donna a letter, written in classical Arabic script and addressed to the mayor of the Iranian village where Shalala would live. The letter informed the mayor that Shalala's family expected her to be treated well and to return safely to Cleveland.

Shalala later credited her Peace Corps experience with profoundly affecting her life, and with teaching her lessons that she later would use in her career. In a 1995 speech she described the importance of her two years in Iran:

> Peace Corps was my dusty pathway to adulthood. It taught me about myself and about the world. It was my coming of age. I learned about real leadership as I watched the village leaders try to improve the lives of families in remote, desperate places. I learned to appreciate other cultures . . . and respect other values. I learned patience. . . . And through it all, I learned pragmatism.

A CAREER IN ACADEMIA

In 1964 Shalala returned from Iran. Within six years, she had earned both her master's and doctorate degrees from the Maxwell School of Citizenship and Public Affairs at Syracuse University, in New York. She moved to New York City to assume teaching positions, first at Baruch College and later at Columbia University.

But it soon became clear that Shalala's skills were not limited to the classroom setting. Although she enjoyed teaching about public policy, she was also fascinated with how to make public institutions and organizations work more effectively.

In 1975, at the age of just 34, Shalala was selected to serve as treasurer of the Municipal Assistance Corporation (MAC) of New York. New York City was suffering from a severe fiscal crisis and many people feared that the city would have to declare bankruptcy. Public services were being cut back, city employees laid off, and desperately needed repairs to roads and schools

cancelled. MAC was a public institution that was created to find a way out of the crisis. Shalala was successful in helping to devise a plan to save New York from financial collapse.

Shalala's administrative abilities were further recognized in 1980, when she was chosen to be president of Hunter College of the City University of New York. After a successful eight-year tenure, she was asked to serve as chancellor of the University of Wisconsin, in Madison—one of the country's largest public universities.

A POLITICAL CAREER

While carrying out important reforms at the University of Wisconsin—including a significant increase in the number of minority members on the faculty—Shalala also began establishing important political relationships. Hillary Clinton became one of her closest friends. And when Hillary's husband, Bill Clinton, was elected president in 1992, he asked Shalala to serve as Secretary of the Department of Health and Human Services (HHS).

Shalala served as secretary of HHS for all eight years of Clinton's presidency. She was a dynamic and at times controversial leader, and her record of accomplishments is long: She expanded the Head Start Program, which provides preschool education to low-income children. She increased funding for research into acquired immune deficiency syndrome (AIDS). She fought for universal immunizations for children. And she helped to craft the Clinton administration's plan to reform the welfare program.

Shalala also received widespread praise for her ability to manage HHS, a huge government agency with over 60,000 employees across the United States.

◄ CROSS-CURRENTS ►

Donna Shalala and hundreds of other Arab-American women have made significant contributions to American society. In the process they have often had to struggle against discrimination against women. In addition, Arab-American women come from a culture that traditionally does not generally support women's rights. Read about "Women in the Arab World" on page 51.

A RETURN TO THE ACADEMIC LIFE

When the Clinton administration ended in 2001, Shalala returned to academia—and to sunnier climes—as president of the University of Miami. She immediately went to work to raise new funds for the university's research programs and to improve the quality of student life on campus. With her experience in fighting political battles in Washington, Shalala knew how to work closely with the political leadership in the city of Miami.

In June 2008 Shalala was presented with the Presidential Medal of Freedom, the nation's highest civilian award, by George W. Bush.

Although Shalala is a staunch Democrat, her abilities have been widely recognized by Republicans as well. In 2007 President George W. Bush asked her to cochair a special White House Commission to investigate the level and quality of medical care being offered to returning veterans from the war in Iraq. The following year Bush awarded Shalala the Presidential Medal of Freedom. The medal recognizes outstanding service to individuals who have contributed to national security, world peace, or American culture.

CHAPTER FOUR

Paul Orfalea: Kinko's Founder

In 1970 a young college student of Lebanese descent started a small copy shop in Santa Barbara, California, with a $5,000 loan and one Xerox machine. He called the shop Kinko's—the nickname his friends had given him because of his kinky hair. The shop was so small that when he purchased a second copy machine, it had to be placed outside on the sidewalk. No one expected that the little shop in Santa Barbara would grow to become the world's largest business services enterprise. But then, no one had ever expected Paul Orfalea to succeed—no one, that is, except his close-knit and entrepreneurial Arab-American family.

DEFYING DISABILITIES

Paul Orfalea was born November 28, 1947, in Los Angeles, California. Declared "learning disabled" at an early age, he struggled academically—and actually was expelled from several schools.

When Orfalea was growing up in the 1950s and 1960s, people had very little knowledge of conditions such as dyslexia and attention deficit hyperactivity disorder (ADHD), or of how to treat them. Children with these conditions usually fell through the cracks of the educational system, and many with severe dyslexia never learned to read at all. Orfalea was no exception. He struggled to graduate from high school, often relying on friends to do his work. He got through community college and graduated from the University of Southern California in Los Angeles.

But one thing about Orfalea's struggle with learning disabilities *was* exceptional—the support he received from his family, and especially from his strong-willed mother. When Paul was 13, the principal of his school told his mother that the best she could hope for was that "one day, maybe Paul can learn to lay carpet for a living." Paul's mother refused to accept this—she knew how bright and full of life her son was. She and Paul's father encouraged him to accept that success in school does not always translate into success in life. As Orfalea remembers it, "My parents taught me to reject conventional wisdom and to rely on my own deepest instincts."

FAMILY HERITAGE

Orfalea's grandparents had immigrated to the United States from Lebanon and settled in southern California at a time when Los Angeles was still a small city. His maternal grandmother

The Ventura, California-based company Kinko's Inc. was founded in 1970 by the entrepreneurial son of Lebanese immigrants—Paul Orfalea. By the mid-1990s it was the leading retail provider of document copying and business services in the world.

was widowed at an early age and raised her seven children alone while operating a small clothing store. Paul's mother and her siblings worked in the store.

Paul's father also ran a successful clothing business, including a garment factory and a retail store in Hollywood. His mother's childhood experience in the retail business proved very helpful to his father, and Paul often talked about the good example his parents set in running a business. He was also aware that his family's Arab culture placed a great emphasis on entrepreneurship. Orfalea once told an interviewer:

Kinko's chairman and founder Paul Orfalea sold the business in 2004 for $2.4 billion.

My family is Lebanese, and when we were growing up, I never knew anybody who had a job—everyone always had their own business. . . . That's the way we were brought up; you work for yourself. The two things my mother always stressed were saving enough money so you can start a business and getting enough sleep.

KINKO'S SOARS

With his parent's support and encouragement, Orfalea seized the opportunity to open his business when he realized that students at UCSB had no place except for the university library to make copies. Over the next five years, Orfalea opened 24 Kinko's stores throughout California. By 1980 there were 80 stores in college towns across America.

Orfalea managed his rapidly growing company in unique ways, largely due to his need to compensate for what others had termed his "disabilities." Reading was very difficult for him, so he preferred to leave the office and travel from store to store. There, he chatted with the managers and the customers and gained a real feel for how each store was performing. He also insisted on running individual stores as partnerships in which store employees shared in the profits. Having a stake in the company's success gave them an incentive to provide excellent customer service.

◀ CROSS-CURRENTS ▶

Paul Orfalea has developed some sayings, or aphorisms, that reflect his unique way of seeing the world. To read some of "Orfalea's Aphorisms," turn to page 52.

Orfalea ran his company almost by instinct, not by poring over reports and analyses. Unlike many hard-driven corporate chief executive officers, Orfalea always took vacations with his wife and children: He believed that he needed to get away from the day-to-day grind in order to think creatively and come up with new innovations. Over time, Orfalea began to see that his learning "disorders" were in fact "learning opportunities."

By 2000 Kinko's had expanded internationally and included more than a thousand stores. Orfalea began to think that there were other things he wanted to do in life, so in 2004 he sold Kinko's and its 1,500 stores to FedEx, the express delivery company, which renamed the stores FedEx Kinko's.

A BUSY "RETIREMENT"

Orfalea could have retired for the rest of his life after selling Kinko's. Instead he used some of the money from the sale of the company to establish a foundation that gives grants to educators and institutions to improve the understanding of learning disorders (what Orfalea terms "learning differences"). Although Orfalea always struggled in school, he is a strong believer in education, and has donated both his time and money to a number of universities.

Paul Orfalea: Kinko's Founder

Orfalea and the Orfalea Family Foundation provided funding to establish the Orfalea Center for Global and International Studies at University of California, Santa Barbara. Former U.S. president Bill Clinton (left) participated in a program with Orfalea in inaugurating the new center in October 2006.

Orfalea's inspiring life story has been widely recognized, and he has won numerous awards and honors. But one of the most special acknowledgements of Orfalea's career and his heritage was the honorary doctoral degree he was awarded by the Lebanese American University at a ceremony in Beirut, Lebanon.

CHAPTER FIVE

Mitch Daniels: State Governor

A first generation Syrian-American, Mitch Daniels was sworn in as the 49th governor of the state of Indiana in 2005. The Republican politician is a former White House budget director, who served during the administration of President George W. Bush.

FAMILY ROOTS

Mitchell Elias Daniels, Jr., was born on April 7, 1949, in the small town of Monongahela, nestled in the mountains of western Pennsylvania. The mines and factories in that region attracted thousands of Arab immigrants during the early 20th century. Most of them were Christians from what is today Lebanon and Syria. One of those families—whose name was Americanized to Daniels—immigrated to the United States from a small mountain town along the Lebanese-Syrian border.

Mitchell Elias Daniels, Sr., and his wife, Dorothy, joined many other Arab families

The son of Syrian immigrants, Mitch Daniels was elected governor of Indiana in 2004.

that had settled in Monongahela. The town is located along the Monongahela River, about 17 miles southwest of the big industrial city of Pittsburgh. Most Arab immigrants to the Monongahela area pursued the retail trade. They started with peddling, but eventually opened food stores and other businesses.

Mitch Daniels, Sr., was a World War II veteran who returned home after the war to pursue a career as a pharmaceutical salesman for a major drug company. His job took him to Georgia for several years and eventually to an executive position with a drug company in Indiana when Mitch was 10 years old.

Like the children of many immigrants, Mitch was encouraged—and expected—to work hard at school. In 1967, when he graduated from North Central High School, in Indianapolis, he was hailed as Indiana's top high school graduate. Named by President Lyndon Johnson as a Presidential Scholar, Daniels became the first Arab American to win the nation's highest honor for high school students.

THE POLITICAL "BUG" BITES

Young Mitch Daniels's trip to Washington to accept the Presidential Scholar award whetted his appetite for politics and public service. The teen enrolled in Princeton University's prestigious Woodrow Wilson School of Public and International Affairs, graduating in 1971.

Daniels then went to work for the mayor of Indianapolis, Richard Lugar, and followed him to Washington when Lugar was elected to the U.S. Senate. While working full-time for Senator Lugar, Daniels attended Georgetown University law school at night. He received his law degree in 1979.

Impressed by the work Daniels was doing for Senator Lugar, President Ronald Reagan offered him a senior job in the White House in 1985. Two years later, with the Reagan administration coming to an end, Daniels left his White House job and returned to Indianapolis.

Following in the footsteps of his father, Daniels joined Indiana-based Eli Lilly and Company, one of the world's largest drug manufacturers. By 1997 the hard-working Daniels had risen to become head of Eli Lilly's corporate strategy, an extremely important role in a company that must be constantly developing new drugs in order to remain a leader in its field.

Despite his success in the corporate world, Daniels had caught the political "bug" on his first trip to Washington. When George W. Bush was elected president in 2004, Daniels accepted his offer to return to Washington as head of the White House Office of Management and Budget (OMB).

This office is one of the most powerful offices in the federal Government. OMB prepares the President's annual budget—it determines how federal dollars will be spent and which government programs will get the most money. After the terrorist attacks of September 11, 2001, one of Daniels's biggest tasks was determining how the federal government would allocate its resources to fight international terrorism and ensure the country's safety.

In his position as director of the Office of Management and Budget (OMB), Daniels explains parts of President Bush's tax proposal during a February 2001 briefing in Washington.

GOVERNOR DANIELS

Daniels headed OMB until 2003. After serving on the staff of a U.S. senator and in two White House administrations, Daniels felt ready to run for political office himself. And he aimed high: Mitch Daniels wanted to be governor of Indiana. His opponent in the 2004 race for Indiana governor was an incumbent governor, Joe Kiernan.

Incumbents usually have an advantage over challengers. But Daniels was not deterred. He spent over a year traveling across Indiana in a large white recreational vehicle (RV) that was plastered with his campaign's slogan—"My Man Mitch." He visited every single one of Indiana's 92 counties at least three times, and stopped in many small towns that had never experienced a campaign visit before. Daniels was running as a Republican, but he campaigned actively for the support of Democrats as well.

Indiana governor Daniels (front, left) tours flood damage in the town of Edwardsport in June 2008. After heavy rains caused serious flooding across central and southern Indiana, he traveled to the hardest-hit areas to assess damage and check on local and state relief efforts.

The tireless campaigning paid off—Daniels won the election with 54 percent of the vote. Just a few months before the November election that made him governor, his father died, in August 2004. The new governor said that the values that his family instilled in him—hard work, education, public service and ambition—were the factors that led to his success.

In 2007 Daniels expressed satisfaction with his accomplishments when he told a group of university students that his administration had brought about change for the state of Indiana. These goals, he said, included balancing the state budget and reducing state spending. He explained:

> I only ran for the job because I thought there were a lot of things that had been let slide in this state; I was restless watching this state slip behind by every indicator. . . . We laid it all out there and we've added some things to that agenda as we've gone along, of course, but we have gone for it.

In the November 2008 gubernatorial elections, Daniels defeated Democratic challenger Jill Long Thompson to earn a second term as governor of Indiana.

◀ CROSS-CURRENTS ▶

Mitch Daniels is not the first Arab American to serve as state governor. To learn more about the many other U.S. politicians who are of Arab heritage, turn to page 53.

CHAPTER SIX

Elias Zerhouni: NIH Director

About 30 years after Algerian immigrant Elias Zerhouni arrived in the United States with less than $400 to his name, the physician was selected to serve as director of the National Institutes of Health (NIH). Part of the U.S. Department of Health and Human services, the NIH is a multi-billion dollar research institution. The appointment of Zerhouni in 2002 made him one of the leaders of America's medical research efforts.

FAMILY ROOTS

Elias A. Zerhouni was born in April 12, 1951, in Nedroma, an ancient town of western Algeria situated at the foot of mountains and known for its beautiful 12th-century Islamic mosque. At the time, Algeria was a colony of France, and Nedroma was an important regional center for agriculture and commerce.

Elias was the fifth brother in a family of seven boys. His father was a math and physics teacher, which made him an important and respected figure in the town, for most Algerians were illiterate. Zerhouni has acknowledged "growing up in a family with a teacher as a father made me worship education."

CHILDHOOD IN THE MIDST OF WAR

When Elias was two, his family moved to Algiers, the nation's capital. Algiers was a coastal city whose ancient quarter—known in Arabic as the *casbah*—was a maze of narrow streets and alleys.

Just after the Zerhouni family arrived in Algiers, the city entered a period of political unrest and violence. In 1954 Algerian nationalists had started an uprising to free their country from 130 years of French rule. The French army responded harshly, and Algiers experienced an extended period of urban warfare that became known as the Battle of Algiers. In 1962 the French agreed to withdraw from Algeria and grant the country its independence, but not before several hundred thousand Algerians had been killed in years of fighting.

Elias still managed to attend school during this difficult and violent period and he was a diligent student. He also became a competitive swimmer, and while still in high school he was invited to join Algeria's national swim team. After completing high school Elias enrolled at the city's University of Algiers. Inspired by his physician uncle, he planned to study medicine.

A BOLD DECISION

In 1975, after Zerhouni received his medical degree with a specialty in radiology, he knew that he had many options. He could stay in Algeria and work for the state-run health system; he could move to Europe, where many Algerians had emigrated; or he could seek a more challenging path.

In the mid-1970s Algeria was ruled by a military-backed socialist government that was allied with the Soviet Union. Thanks to its large reserves of oil and natural gas, it was a country with great potential but the bloody war of independence had destroyed much of the country's infrastructure. Moreover, the socialist government ruled authoritatively. It took control of most of Algeria's businesses, prohibited a free press, and stifled opposition voices. Although Algeria was now a free and independent country, it was

Elias Zerhouni stands in front of National Institutes of Health (NIH) headquarters in Bethesda, Maryland. The Algerian-born U.S. citizen served as director of NIH from 2002 to 2008.

Elias Zerhouni: NIH Director

not a pleasant place to live—especially for an ambitious and intelligent young physician.

Zerhouni decided to immigrate to the United States, a choice that very few Algerians took. For one thing, few Algerians spoke English—most spoke French and Arabic. Moreover, the country's government was anti-American. But Zerhouni's physician uncle, who had lived for many years in Switzerland and knew much of the world, convinced him that moving to the United States was his best option. "My uncle said the only country that would treat me well and was truly visionary was America," Zerhouni later recalled. "He said I needed to find a way to go there."

Shortly before leaving Algeria, Zerhouni married fellow medical school classmate Nadia Azza, whom he had first met when she also qualified for the national team as a competitive swimmer. The couple settled in Baltimore, Maryland, where Elias was to start his residency in diagnostic radiology at Johns Hopkins University. Zerhouni described the experience:

> I had exactly $369 and I spoke broken English. When I came here with my wife we didn't think we would be able to stay long. I was a qualified doctor so I worked in the emergency room on night shift, which nobody wanted. But you know what? It was the best thing I did. It gave me a training that I couldn't have hoped to get anywhere else.

CLIMBING THE LADDER OF SUCCESS

Just four years after arriving in the United States, Zerhouni was invited to join the faculty of Johns Hopkins University Medical School as an assistant professor. After a stint teaching at Eastern Virginia Medical School from 1981 to 1985, he returned to Johns Hopkins as an associate professor and then full professor in the department of radiology. He was highly respected by both his students and his colleagues, and in 1996 was appointed chairman of the radiology department at Johns Hopkins.

In the interim, Elias and Nadia Zerhouni, who was trained as a pediatrician, established a home in Baltimore and raised three children, all of whom were born in the United States. His children, while aware of their heritage, have followed the pattern of assimilation that most children of immigrants follow. "I have three kids who were born here, terrific Americans," Zerhouni said. "My kids are probably 90 percent American and 10 percent Algerian."

◀ CROSS-CURRENTS ▶

Elias Zerhouni became a naturalized citizen of the United States in 1990. To learn more about the requirements foreign-born immigrants need to fulfill to become U.S. citizens, turn to page 53.

By 2002 Zerhouni had risen to become vice-dean of the entire Johns Hopkins Medical School, where he continued to teach students the science of radiology. He had proven to be both a brilliant scientist and teacher, as well a confident leader and administrator. In May 2002 Zerhouni got a phone call from the White House: President George W. Bush wanted him to serve as director of the National Institutes of Health.

Zerhouni shakes hands with George W. Bush during the president's visit to the National Institutes of Health in January 2005.

A NEW CHALLENGE

NIH consists of 27 individual institutes and centers, employs nearly 18,000 people and operates with a $30 billion budget. Heading such a huge institution is no easy task, but Zerhouni was up to the challenge. He instituted a number of new programs and reforms in the six years that he directed NIH. One of his most important initiatives was a major investigation into the causes and cures of obesity, a serious health care problem in the United States that often begins in childhood.

Zerhouni also changed a previous policy in order to allow public access to NIH research publications, which are now available on the NIH Web site. This allows Americans who suffer from rare diseases to access information on the latest research and treatments. Doctors from all over the world can also access potentially life-saving information.

In April 2008 French president Nicolas Sarkozy awards Elias A. Zerhouni the French National Order of the Legion of Honor, the highest decoration in France. Looking on is the NIH director's wife, Nadia Zerhouni.

Elias Zerhouni's successful career in the United States was an important accomplishment not only for Arab Americans, but for Muslim Americans as well. Never before had a Muslim American been appointed to such a high federal government position. Zerhouni credits the United States for providing him the opportunity despite the discrimination against Muslims that followed the September 11 terrorist attacks. He explains:

> I am an Arab-American Muslim, and I am serving my country and doing it with all my heart. I strongly believe that one of the strongest core values of our country is that it is not who you are that determines where you go; it is what you've done and what you have accomplished.

In September 2008 Zerhouni announced he was stepping down from the position of NIH director. He explained that he would pursue writing projects and explore other professional opportunities.

CHAPTER SEVEN

Bobby Rahal: Race Car Driving Legend

Bobby Rahal has centered his life around cars. He gained renown in the 1980s and 1990s as a winning auto racing driver. Although now retired as a driver, he has remained active in the sport. With talk show host and television and film producer David Letterman, he owns Rahal Letterman Racing, an auto racing team that competes in the IndyCar Series.

IMMIGRANT ROOTS

One of the largest communities of Arab Americans lives in the area around Cleveland, Ohio. Arab immigrants were attracted to the city and its suburbs in the early 20th century, a period when the area's industrial-based economy was booming. A number of Arab families settled in the small town of Medina, about 30 miles south of Cleveland. They may have been attracted to Medina by the fact that the word *medina* in Arabic means "city." (Medina was founded in 1816, so its name pre-dates the establishment of its Arab community.)

One of the early families to settle in Medina was the Rahal family, which emigrated from the small Lebanese village of Aitaneet. Like many Arab immigrants, the Rahals were drawn to the retail trades and establishing their own businesses. Mike Rahal, whose father had immigrated to Medina, served in the U.S. Navy during World War II.

After the war and college, Mike Rahal went to work for an uncle's fruit juice business. Later he established his own successful wholesale fruit and frozen foods business that supplied local restaurants and grocery stores. Mike later observed that many Lebanese became entrepreneurs: "It was almost an article of faith," he said, "that the Arab business people first sold linens and rags from house to house and progressed from there to the next level of enterprise."

While Mike succeeded in the wholesale food business, his real passion was racing sports cars. He never saw auto racing as a career; to Mike Rahal, it was a hobby he pursued on weekends at local race tracks. Mike's son, Bobby, would choose a different direction.

Robert "Bobby" Rahal has gained fame as a championship race car driver and owner of the auto racing team Rahal Letterman Racing.

RACING FEVER

Robert "Bobby" Woodward Rahal was born January 10, 1953, in Medina. He grew up helping his father repair race cars. And he spent his weekends watching his father compete on the track. By the age of 14, Bobby was a valued member of his father's pit crew.

Although auto racing played a huge part in Bobby Rahal's early life, he never imagined that he would one day race cars for a living. In his family, Bobby was taught to value education and the professions. As he described it:

> I grew up around cars in general. There were always race cars around our house. . . . We all got involved in it, but there was never any thought of my being a professional driver. It was assumed I would go through high school and then college, and then I would have a career. If you wanted to race, well, you know, you would be a weekend warrior.

Bobby attended Denison College, in Granville, Ohio. After graduating with a bachelor's degree in history, he went to work for an advertising agency in Chicago. But the lure of the racetrack was strong, and Rahal's success in weekend racing fueled his ambition: He was determined to make car racing more than just a hobby.

A BRILLIANT CAREER

Rahal liked to race open-wheel cars, also commonly known as Indy cars and Formula One cars. These are one-seater race cars with a tiny cockpit for the driver and no top. The wheels are located outside the main body of the car. Open-wheel cars, which are designed for racing, regularly reach speeds of over 200 miles per hour.

At age 25 Rahal entered his first Grand Prix race ("Grand Prix" refers to major international competitions), and his career in motor sports had begun. In 1982, at the age of 29, he participated in his first Indianapolis 500 race, one of motor sports' most prestigious events. Over the next 17 years, Rahal won

24 major races, including the 1986 Indianapolis 500 before a crowd of more than 300,000 people and a national television audience. His 1986 Indy 500 victory also broke the record for highest average speed during a 500-mile race—over 170 miles per hour.

An exuberant Rahal celebrates winning the Indianapolis 500 on May 31, 1986.

During his 21 years of active racing, Bobby Rahal became a household name among motor sports enthusiasts. He also became very wealthy from the many monetary prizes he received for racing victories. Successful and well-known race car drivers also are in a position to sell sponsorships—funds provided by big companies to underwrite racing expenses. By the time he retired from racing in 1999, Rahal had earned over $16 million in victory prizes alone.

A NEW LIFE

But Rahal did not retire to a life of leisure—although he had the money to do so. Instead, he started two new highly

During practice at the Indianapolis Motor Speedway, Rahal gives some words of encouragement to Indy Racing League driver Danica Patrick, who in 2005 was driving for Rahal Letterman Racing.

successful business: One is the Rahal Automotive Group, a company that owns automobile dealerships throughout western and central Pennsylvania. The other is Rahal Letterman Racing, a company that owns, maintains and races open-wheel race cars. Rahal's partner in Rahal Letterman Racing is late-night television personality David Letterman.

Bobby Rahal accomplished what most people only dream of: He turned his passion—racing cars—into an enormously successful career and business enterprise. And Rahal has shared the fruits of his success with those less fortunate. The Bobby Rahal Foundation has donated millions of dollars to charities, with a focus on children's health.

◄ CROSS-CURRENTS ►

Cross-Currents: Bobby Rahal and his wife Debi are the parents of two sons, Jarrad and Graham Robert, and two daughters, Michaela and Samantha. One of them has followed Bobby into the career of professional race car driver. To learn more, turn to page 54.

CHAPTER EIGHT

Paula Abdul: Television Personality

Pop singer and dancer Paula Abdul has won awards for her recordings and work as a choreographer, actress, and television personality. The daughter of a Syrian father, she is best known today as one of the judges on the popular television show *American Idol*.

American Idol judge Paula Abdul waves to fans while onstage during the grand finale of the program's seventh season, filmed in May 2008 in Los Angeles, California.

AN UNUSUAL STORY

The course that Paula Abdul's family took to the United States was different from that of most Arab immigrants. Abdul's father, Harry, was born in Syria. His family moved first to Lebanon and eventually to Brazil, where Harry grew up and where the Abdul family established a livestock trading business. In the 1950s Harry decided to immigrate to the United States, where he settled in the Los Angeles area. He started a sand and gravel business that served the booming southern California construction industry. His wife, Lorraine, was from Canada. Their daughter, Paula Julie Abdul, was born in San Fernando, California, on June 19, 1962.

The Abduls are Jewish. Many people are unaware that the Arab world was once home to a large Jewish community, which had thrived in Arab lands since ancient times. It is important to remember that Arab refers to an ethnicity and a cultural identification, not a religion. And just as there are Muslim and Christian Arabs, there also are Jewish Arabs—people who practice the Jewish religion but who share their neighbors' language, cuisine, and social customs.

◀ CROSS-CURRENTS ▶

People of the Jewish faith have been a part of the Arab world since ancient times. However, during the 20th century, most emigrated from their homeland. For more information, turn to page 55.

LOVE OF DANCE

Almost as soon as she could walk, Paula Abdul fell in love with dancing. By age eight, she was taking dance lessons. At Van Nuys High School, in Los Angeles, she was a member of the cheerleading team, played flute in the school band, and was an honor student. Her interest in dance, combined with her experience on the cheerleading team, led to an interest in choreography—the art of planning and arranging dance movements.

Abdul enrolled at California State University, at Northridge, with the intention of studying broadcasting. But at the same time she began to explore opportunities in choreography. Her first big break came when she was offered the position of head cheerleader and choreographer for the Los Angeles Lakers professional basketball team. Soon after, she left school and pursued various choreography projects. During the 1980s she choreographed music videos for a number of entertainers, including pop star Michael Jackson, singer Janet Jackson, musician Prince, and rock band ZZ Top.

Abdul began winning jobs to develop dance scenes for Hollywood films and television shows; in 1989 she won an Emmy Award—the television industry's highest honor—for her television work in choreography. She even choreographed and danced in a television commercial for Diet Coke.

A MUSICAL CAREER

Abdul's talents were not limited to dance and choreography—she also could sing. Dipping into her savings, she made a professionally produced demo tape and sent it to record producers. In 1988 she released her first album, *Forever Your Girl*, which hit number one on the charts. It was followed in the early 1990s by two more albums.

Abdul holds American Music Awards for Favorite Pop/Rock Female Artist and Favorite Dance Artist, which she won in January 1990. Her album Forever Your Girl *was also nominated as Favorite Pop/Rock Album, but did not win.*

Almost overnight Paula Abdul became a pop star as her dance-oriented music rose to the top of the charts. In 1995 she released her fourth album, *Head Over Heels*, which included a song using traditional Middle Eastern musical instruments. She was accompanied in "My Love Is for Real" by singer Ofra Haza, a woman of Yemenite Jewish ancestry who was a successful star in Israel. The music video that accompanied the song was popular worldwide.

DIFFICULT TIMES

Despite her popularity, Abdul was going through difficult times. Pop stars and especially dancers are under tremendous pressure to look good—which generally means to look *thin*. Sometimes, this pressure and the accompanying anxiety can lead to serious problems. In 1995 Abdul admitted in a television interview that she had suffered for 17 years from bulimia, a serious eating disorder. People with the disorder eat large quantities of food, which they then purge from their bodies so they do not gain weight.

By the time she admitted in the interview to having bulimia, Abdul had already sought treatment. She later became a spokesperson for the National Eating Disorders Association. In that role, she recorded public service announcements to educate other young women of the dangers of eating disorders and urge them to get help.

In the late 1990s Abdul's career had reached a plateau. Her fourth album did not sell as well as her earlier ones, and dance-oriented music was losing popularity. Two failed marriages—along with her bulimia—were contributing to a difficult period in her life.

THE *IDOL* ERA

Paula Abdul needed another break, and it came in 2002 when she was asked to be one of the judges for a new reality television show called *American Idol*. The show was based on a

similar show that had been a big hit in Britain, but no one knew whether U.S. audiences would watch an American version of the program.

Abdul was paired with fellow judges Simon Cowell and Randy Jackson. Their job was to narrow down the number of initial amateur singing contestants. Later on in the program, the judges critiqued the performances of the singers while television audiences voted on who advanced in the competition.

First broadcast in June 2002, *American Idol* became a huge success, watched by millions of viewers—and Abdul's career got a renewed boost. She was regarded by many as the kindest of the three judges—the one who always offered her critique in as gentle a way as possible. She says she has strong empathy for others, telling one interviewer: "I know my life purpose: having the uncanny ability to tap into the heartstrings of people and make them feel they'll be OK."

American Idol judges for the 2008 season (left to right): Simon Cowell, Kara DioGuardi, Paula Abdul, and Randy Jackson.

Paula Abdul: Television Personality

ATTITUDES TOWARD IMMIGRATION

The Gallup organization surveys people around the world to determine public opinion regarding various political, social, and economic issues. One issue that Gallup has researched over the years is immigration to the United States. In general, Americans have a positive view of immigration, reports the Gallup Web site:

Three in four [Americans] have consistently said it has been good for the United States in the past, and a majority says it is good for the nation today. However, Americans still seem interested in limiting the amount of immigration.

When asked in a July 2008 Gallup survey about the level of immigration into the United States, 39 percent of Americans favored decreasing the number of immigrants allowed into the country, a decrease from 45 percent a year earlier. However, only 18 percent believe it should be increased.

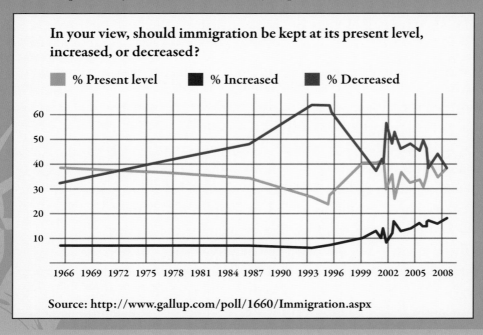

In your view, should immigration be kept at its present level, increased, or decreased?

■ % Present level   ■ % Increased   ■ % Decreased

Source: http://www.gallup.com/poll/1660/Immigration.aspx

WOMEN IN THE ARAB WORLD

Arab-American women from both Arab Muslim and Arab Christian families come from a culture that traditionally has not generally supported women's rights and opportunities. Immigrants from the Arab world often bring their cultural attitudes with them and in both Muslim and Christian societies, women are traditionally members of patriarchal families. These families sometimes faced internal conflict after immigrating to the United States, where women generally had greater freedom.

The rights of women in the Arab world varies from country to country. In Saudi Arabia, a conservative and traditional Muslim nation, women are required to wear veils when in public and are banned from certain privileges, such as the right to drive a car. In contrast, in the North African nation of Tunisia women make up nearly 25 percent of the elected national parliament. In countries such as Egypt, Lebanon, and Jordan, women frequently hold top positions in business and government. Most Arab countries allow women to vote in elections, although in some more traditional nations they may vote only in local races.

Traditionally, Arab women have not enjoyed the same access to education as men. This, however, is beginning to slowly change. Increasingly, women are forming organizations in Arab countries to help fight for more freedoms and equal rights.

Arab women buying apples at a street market in Palmyra, Syria.

THE "OLD COUNTRY"

Millions of people have immigrated to the United States in order to escape terrible conditions in their native countries. They may be fleeing poverty and starvation or a repressive government. America has long symbolized freedom and opportunity for immigrants seeking a better future.

Once they settle in the United States, some immigrants turn their backs on their native country. They may associate their earlier lives with pain and suffering, or they may simply want to assimilate into the American culture as quickly as possible. But some immigrants remain connected to their native country, either because family members still live there or because they want to hold on to aspects of their culture and heritage—and pass them on to their children.

Ralph Nader's parents made sure that their son understood his roots and the importance of cultural traditions. When Nader was a young boy, his mother took him and his three siblings on a yearlong trip to Lebanon. (Nader's father remained at home to run the family business.) Rose Nader traveled with her children to her ancestral village deep in the mountains of Lebanon, where the children met members of her extended family.

In his book *The Seventeen Traditions* Nader described the visit and the powerful impact it had on him: "We learned of the struggles of my great-grandparents' generation, and absorbed the cultural history of custom, myth, folklore, festivities, food, humor and religion," he explained.

ORFALEA'S APHORISMS

During his life and career Paul Orfalea has developed some sayings, or aphorisms, that reflect his unique way of seeing the world. Here are a few of Orfalea's aphorisms:
- Learn to please yourself, not others.
- Success is more about your imagination than anything else.
- I've always valued thinking hard over working hard.
- In business, and in life, you have to come to terms with the fact that life is uncertain.
- The best thing in life is making something out of nothing. The imagination is your only limiting factor.
- The art of life is to rediscover who you are every day.
- It's not the things you do, but the things you don't do that drive you crazy.
- The only true victories in life are victories over ourselves.
- It's taken me my whole life to figure out that I don't have all the answers.
- You're only as good as your dreams.

OTHER ARAB-AMERICAN POLITICIANS

When he was elected governor of Indiana in 2004, Mitch Daniels joined a distinguished list of Arab Americans who have succeeded in the political arena. Other Arab Americans who have served as state governor are Victor Atiyeh and John Sununu. Atiyeh, who was the first Arab American elected to a statewide office, served as governor of Oregon from 1979 to 1987. John Sununu was elected governor of New Hampshire in 1983 and later served as White House Chief of Staff to President George H. W. Bush.

Many Arab Americans have been members of the U.S. Congress. The former New Hampshire governor's son, John Sununu, Jr., represented that state as senator. George Mitchell was a U.S. senator from Maine and rose to become Senate Majority Leader. He later helped to negotiate an historic peace agreement in Northern Ireland on behalf of President Bill Clinton. During the 1980s, both of South Dakota's U.S. senators were Arab Americans: James Abourezk and James Abdnor. Spencer Abraham was elected to the U.S. Senate from Michigan and later served as U.S. Secretary of Energy. Several Arab Americans have served in the U.S. House of Representatives, and dozens have been successful in local politics.

Almost all of the Arab Americans who have won political office in the United States have been Christians from families that immigrated from Lebanon and Syria during the first wave of Arab immigration. Muslim Arab Americans, however, are increasingly becoming involved in politics.

BECOMING A U.S. CITIZEN

After a foreign-born immigrant has lived continuously in the United States for a minimum of five years, he or she can take steps to become a "naturalized citizen." That is, the immigrant can obtain the same rights of citizenship as those belonging to someone who was born in the United States.

The applicant must be a lawful, permanent resident who is over the age of 18 and has passed a citizenship exam. Spouses of U.S. citizens can become naturalized citizens after three years. Children who are immigrants usually become citizens when their parents are naturalized.

According to the *2000 Census Brief on the Foreign-Born Population in the United States*, about 40.3 percent of the foreign-born population in the United States are naturalized citizens. Elias Zerhouni, who came to the United States in 1975, is among them, having become a naturalized citizen in 1990. "I've spent more than half of my life here," Zerhouni says, "so now I feel as American as I feel Algerian."

GRAHAM RAHAL

With a world-famous racing father and a grandfather whose life passion was race cars, is it any surprise that Bobby Rahal's son Graham, born in 1989, also would catch racing fever? Graham entered his first professional race in 2004—at the age of just 15. His first professional victory came one year later, and he quickly established himself as a serious competitor in the world of motor sports.

In 2006 Graham won five major races. But the highlight of that year for young Graham came when he competed in an international Grand Prix race held in Mexico as a driver for A1 Team Lebanon, a racing team based in his family's ancestral home country.

When Graham was named to A1 Team Lebanon, he remarked: "This is an exciting opportunity for me. I've always recognised my Lebanese roots, so to compete for the country of my ancestry is very special." Graham's proud father added, "I'm very proud of our Lebanese heritage and this unique opportunity for my son to represent not just Lebanon and the Arab world, but the Lebanese community in the United States."

In April 2008, at age 19, Graham Rahal became the youngest open-wheel race winner at the Honda Grand Prix of St. Petersburg, in Florida.

JEWS OF THE ARAB WORLD

Jews have lived in Arab lands since ancient times. Even after the Islamic religion became the dominant religion in the Middle East, around the 7th century A.D., sizable Jewish and Christian communities continued to exist and thrive. However, both Jews and Christians often were discriminated against under Islamic rulers. For example, all non-Muslims had to pay special taxes. And yet in some parts of the Arab world—notably Egypt, Lebanon, Iraq, Tunisia, and Morocco—Jews achieved positions of power and influence, and ran successful businesses.

People in Jewish communities throughout the Arab world spoke Arabic, dressed like their fellow countrymen, and ate the same foods. Despite the discrimination they encountered, they considered themselves to be citizens of the countries in which they lived. In other words, they were culturally Arab—just like the Muslim and Christian communities around them.

In 1948, when the state of Israel was founded as a homeland for the Jewish people, Jews in Arab lands were initially reluctant to relocate from their ancient communities. This attitude changed, however, when Arab states rejected the new state of Israel. Several neighboring Arab states fought a war with Israel from 1948 to 1949.

Most of the Arab states at the time were ruled by authoritarian regimes, where there were few civil rights. Local Jewish populations became scapegoats for the official animosity aimed toward Israel. Feeling threatened, hundreds of thousands of Jews in Arab states immigrated to the new state of Israel. Hundreds of thousands of others immigrated to France, Canada, and the United States.

In a few more open Arab countries, the Jewish communities felt safer. Significant-sized Jewish communities continued to live in Morocco, Lebanon, and Tunisia. But gradually over time, members of these communities migrated to Israel and other countries, especially after 1967 when Israel and the Arab states faced off in another war.

In addition to Paula Abdul's family, a number of other prominent Americans are of Arab Jewish descent. The late Edmond Safra, who was born in Lebanon, founded the Bank of New York. Jack Marshall, an award-winning poet and author, is of Iraqi and Syrian heritage, and wrote a fascinating memoir about growing up in a Jewish Arab family. Actor and rapper Khleo Thomas, who starred in the Disney movie *Holes*, has an African-American father and a Moroccan Jewish mother. The mother of comedian Jerry Seinfeld is of Syrian descent.

NOTES

CHAPTER 2

p. 12: "One day, when I was about ten . . ." Ralph Nader, *The Seventeen Traditions* (New York: Harper Collins, 2007), 69.

p. 13: "If we wanted to . . ." Nader, *The Seventeen Traditions*.

p. 17: "Voting for a candidate of one's choice . . ." Henriette Mantel and Steve Skrovan, *An Unreasonable Man* (Documentary film), 2006.

p. 17: "My father used to say . . ." Nader, *The Seventeen Traditions,* 124.

CHAPTER 3

p. 19: "What she lacked in size . . ." Kim Clark, "A Whirlwind's Winning Ways," *U.S. News and World Report*, October 31, 2005.

p. 20: "Peace Corps was my dusty pathway . . ." Donna Shalala, "Donna Shalala's Remarks on Mark Gearan [to the National Peace Corps Association Conference]," August 4, 1995. www.peacecorpsonline.org

CHAPTER 4

p. 25: "one day, maybe Paul can learn . . ." Paul Orfalea, *Copy This!* (New York: Workman Publishing, 2005), xxi.

p. 25: "My parents taught me . . ." Orfalea, *Copy This!* xxii.

p. 26: "My family is Lebanese . . ." Evan Cooper, "Paul Orfalea: West Coast Asset Management Chief and Founder of Kinko's on Entrepreneurial Investing," *Investment News*, March 31, 2008.

CHAPTER 5

p. 33: "I only ran for the job . . ." "'We Have Gone for It,' Indiana Gov. Mitch Daniels Tells DePauw Audience, DePauw University," October 24, 2007. http://www.depauw.edu/news/index.asp?id=20261

CHAPTER 6

p. 34: "growing up in a family . . ." Sylvia Pagán Westphal, "Hold the Dream," *New Scientist*, January 10, 2004.

p. 36: "My uncle said . . ." Westphal, "Hold the Dream."

p. 36: "I had exactly $369 . . ." Westphal, "Hold the Dream."

p. 37: "I have three kids . . ." Westphal, "Hold the Dream."

p. 39: "I am an Arab-American Muslim . . ." Westphal, "Hold the Dream."

CHAPTER 7

p. 41: "it was always the ambition . . ." Quoted in *Atlas F1*, March 14, 2001 (Volume 7, Issue 11).

p. 42: "I grew up around cars . . ." Kirby, Gordon. *Bobby Rahal: The Graceful Champion* (Somerset, U.K.: Haynes Publishing, 1999), 12.

CHAPTER 8

p. 49 "I know my life purpose . . ." Quoted in Tirdad Derakhshani, "Sideshow: Paula Abdul: I'm Not Wack," *Philadelphia Inquirer*, July 8, 2007.

CROSS-CURRENTS

p. 52: "We learned the struggles of my great-grandparents' . . ." *The Seventeen Traditions* (New York: Harper Collins, 2007), 52.

p. 52: "Orfalea's Aphorisms." Orfalea, *Copy This!* 199-203.

p. 53: "I've spent more . . ." Westphal, "Hold the Dream."

p. 54: "This is an exciting opportunity . . ." "Team Lebanon Names Graham Rahal for Final Races," Motorsport.com, February 21, 2006. http://www.motorsport.com/news/article.asp?ID=210364&FS=A1GP

p. 54: "I'm very proud of our Lebanese heritage . . ." "Team Lebanon Names Graham Rahal for Final Races," Motorsport.com.

GLOSSARY

aphorism—a short and instructive saying.

assimilate—to become part of a mainstream society or culture by adopting customs and attitudes.

authoritarian—a form of government in which the leader or leaders hold all the power; the opposite of democracy.

bulimia—a serious eating disorder characterized by gorging followed by vomiting.

cabinet—a president's closest advisors and heads of the various executive Branch agencies.

choreography—the art of designing dance movements.

dyslexia—a learning disorder characterized by difficulty in recognizing words.

emigrate—to move away from one's country to settle in another country or region.

Emmy—an award given by the Academy of Television Arts and Sciences.

entrepreneur—a person who operates a business and aggressively seeks new ventures.

fiscal—pertaining to a government's taxation and spending policies.

illiterate—unable to read or write.

immigrant—a person who comes to live in a new country or region.

incumbent—the person who currently holds a political office.

infrastructure—fundamental elements of a country's economy, such as roads and power plants.

mosque—the Muslim house of worship.

naturalization—the process by which an immigrant becomes a citizen.

patriarchal—a society in which men are socially dominant.

Peace Corps—a U.S. Government agency that sends Americans abroad to help improve lives in underdeveloped countries.

pit crew—the team that supports a race car driver during a race by changing tires, refueling, and carrying out mechanical repairs.

poll—survey, often conducted over the phone, in person, or over the Internet, in which the public's attitudes about specific issues are documented.

radiology—a field of medicine dealing with X-rays, CAT scans, and other diagnostic techniques.

stereotype—a simplified, and often prejudiced, view of a group.

subsistence—meeting basic survival needs.

FURTHER READING

Bayoumi, Moustapha. *How Does It Feel to be a Problem? Being Young and Arab in America.* New York: Penguin Press, 2008.

Hooglund, Eric J., ed. *Crossing the Waters: Arabic-Speaking Immigrants to the United States Before 1940.* Washington: Smithsonian Institution Press, 1987.

Kirby, Gordon. *Bobby Rahal: The Graceful Champion.* Somerset, U.K.: Haynes Publishing, 1999.

Marshall, Jack. *From Baghdad to Brooklyn: Growing up in a Jewish-Arabic Family in Mid-century America.* New York: Coffee House Press, 2005.

Nader, Ralph. *The Seventeen Traditions.* New York: Harper, 2007.

Orfalea, Gregory. *The Arab Americans: A History.* Northampton, MA: Olive Branch Press, 2006.

Orfalea, Paul. *Copy This!* New York: Workman Publishing, 2005.

INTERNET RESOURCES

www.adc.org
The Web site of the American-Arab Anti-Discrimination Committee, which is a civil rights organization that works to defend the rights of people of Arab descent and to promote the Arab culture.

www.arab-american-affairs.net/
The News Circle Publishing house hosts a Web site that contains links to its publications *Arab American Affairs* magazine and the *Arab American Almanac.*

www.arabamericanmuseum.org
The Web site for the Arab American National Museum, located in Dearborn, Michigan. The museum provides information on Arab American history and culture—as well as shared experiences of immigrants and ethnic groups.

www.gallup.com
The Gallup Organization, an international polling institute, provides insights into social issues, politics, sports, entertainment, and other topics through polls and analyses available on its Web site.

www.nih.gov
The Web site of the nation's medical research agency, the National Institutes of Health, features links to information about the NIH, health information, clinical trials, and research studies.

www.rahal.com
The Rahal Letterman Racing Web site provides news and background information on drivers, teams, cars, and schedules.

OTHER SUCCESSFUL ARAB AMERICANS

Joseph Abboud (1950–): Born in Boston, Massachusetts, of a Christian Lebanese family, Abboud is a successful men's and women's clothing designer. He is also the author of a 2004 book on the fashion industry entitled *Threads: My Life Behind the Seams in the High Stakes World of Fashion*.

Gen. John Abizaid (1951–): Born in Coleville, California, to a Lebanese-American father and an American mother, Abiziad became a U.S. Army general who served as commander of U.S. forces in the Middle East. He retired from the military in May 2007.

Rosemary Barkett (1939–): Born in Mexico to parents of Syrian descent, Barkett is the first female judge and Chief Justice to serve on the Supreme Court for the state of Florida.

Michael DeBakey (1908–2008): Born in Lake Charles, Lousiana, to Orthodox Lebanese immigrants, DeBakey became a world-renowned heart surgeon and inventor of medical devices. He also served as director of the Methodist DeBakey Heart and Vascular Center and senior attending surgeon of the Methodist Hospital in Houston, Texas.

Farouk el-Baz (1938–): Born in the town of Zagazig, Egypt, el-Baz earned his advanced degrees in geology in the United States during the 1960s. Subsequently, the Egyptian-American scientist worked with the National Aeronautics and Space Administration (NASA) in planning scientific exploration of the moon during the Apollo project.

Doug Flutie (1962–) A former professional football quarterback in the National Football League and the Canadian Football League, Flutie won college footballs' coveted Heisman Trophy during his senior year at Boston College.

Khalil Gibran (1883–1931): Poet, writer, and philosopher, Gibran is an author whose most famous book, *The Prophet*, has sold millions of copies worldwide.

J. M. Haggar (1892–1987): The founder of the clothing company that bears his name, Haggar expanded his business from the manufacturer of men's pants to a full line of men's and women's clothing.

Army general John Abizaid, as commander of the U.S. Central Command (CENTCOM), briefs reporters at the Pentagon in July 2003.

Sanaa Hamri (1975?–): Born in Tangier, Morocco, this Moroccan-American music video director also directed *Sisterhood of the Traveling Pants 2*.

Robert Khayat (1938–): Born in Moss Point, Mississippi, Khayat was a student and star athlete in baseball and football at the University of Mississippi, in Oxford. During the early 1960s, he played for the Washington Redskins while attending law school. Subsequently he taught as a member of the law school faculty for the University of Mississippi and in 1995 was named its 15th chancellor.

Edward Said (1935–2003): Born in Jerusalem, in what was then known as the British Mandate of Palestine, Said became a refugee living in Egypt after the 1948 Arab-Israeli War. After obtaining his Ph.D. in the United States, he became a professor of literature at Columbia University in 1963. During his life, he became well known as an advocate for Palestinian rights.

Zainab Salbi (1970?–): Born in Baghdad, Iraq, Salbi is an Iraqi-American writer and activist who speaks out against violence against women. She is the cofounder and president of Women for Women International, an organization working to help women survivors of wars around the world.

Tom Shadyac (1958–): Born in Falls Church, Virginia, to Lebanese parents, Shadyac is a Hollywood director and producer of comedy films such as *Evan Almighty* and *I Now Pronounce You Chuck and Larry*.

Tony Shalhoub (1953–): Actor and star of the NBC television series *Monk*, Shalboub is the winner of three Emmy Awards for Outstanding Lead Actor in a television comedy.

Helen Thomas (1920–): Born in Winchester, Kentucky, to Lebanese immigrant parents, Thomas

A bust of world-renowned heart surgeon Michael DeBakey stands in Methodist Hospital, Houston, Texas.

is a legendary print journalist and best-selling author. She worked for more than 50 years covering Washington, D.C., politics and in 1974 became the first woman to serve as bureau chief for a news wire service—a post she held for more than 25 years.

Ahmed Zewail (1946–): Born in Damanhur, Egypt, Zewail came to the United States in the 1960s to further his education. A professor at the California Institute of Technology since 1976, he is also the winner of the 1999 Nobel Prize in chemistry.

John Zogby (1948–): The son of Lebanese immigrants, John Zogby is widely regarded as the preeminent political pollster in America. He is the founder and president of Zogby International, a phone and Internet polling firm.

Other Successful Arab Americans

INDEX

PICTURE CREDITS

ABOUT THE AUTHOR

Dr. William Mark Habeeb is a writer and consultant who specializes in Middle East politics and has traveled to many countries in that region. He has researched the history of Arab communities in the American South. Dr. Habeeb's father immigrated to the United States from Lebanon in 1920.